THE AUTHOR

Tim Crouch

THE AUTHOR

OBERON BOOKS
LONDON

WWW.OBERONBOOKS.COM

First published in 2009 by Oberon Books Ltd
521 Caledonian Road, London N7 9RH
Tel: +44 (0) 20 7607 3637 / Fax: +44 (0) 20 7607 3629
e-mail: info@oberonbooks.com
www.oberonbooks.com

Reprinted in 2010, 2011, 2013, 2015, 2016 (twice)

A catalogue record for this book is available from the British
Library.

PB ISBN: 9781840029505
E ISBN: 9781849435512

Cover illustration by Julia Collins

Printed and bound by 4Edge Limited, Hockley, Essex, UK.

Dedicated to the memory of John Ringham, actor.

THANKS

Dan Jones – for the vouchers. Camilla Harrisson, Maja Bugge, John Retallack, Diane Borger, Aideen Howard, Francisco Frazao, Mark Russell, Lisa Wolfe, Hannah Ringham, Fee Ringham, Adrian Howells, Kate Horton, Dominic Cooke, Peter Chrisp, Pam and Colin Crouch, Julia, Nel, Owen and Joe.

Commissioned by the Royal Court Theatre

Premiered at the Jerwood Theatre Upstairs, Royal Court
Theatre, London, 23 September 2009

Performed by Tim Crouch, Adrian Howells, Vic Llewellyn,
Esther Smith

Co-directed by Karl James and Andy Smith
Lighting design by Matt Drury
Sound by Ben and Max Ringham

In a subsequent tour, the part originated by Adrian Howells
was taken by Chris Goode.

Characters

ADRIAN

TIM

VIC

ESTHER

The Author is set in the Jerwood Theatre Upstairs at the Royal Court Theatre – even when it's performed elsewhere.

This is a play that happens inside its audience. As the audience enter the space, they encounter two banks of seating, facing each other, comfortably spaced apart but with no 'stage' in between. This must not be a confrontational configuration. The request the play makes is for us to be okay about ourselves, to gently see ourselves and ourselves seeing. There should be plenty of warm, open space in the play. The audience should be beautifully lit and cared for. When the audience is asked questions, these are direct questions that the audience are more than welcome to answer – but under no pressure to do so.

The actors are unspectacularly seated throughout the audience. The sometimes thwarted desire for sections of the audience to see certain actors is a dynamic of 'wanting to see' that is presented by the narrative. It is hoped that the audience will eventually feel encouraged to dispose of the need to look at whoever is speaking and enjoy their own company.

The names of the characters in this text are the names of the actors playing them for the Royal Court premiere. If the actors change, then the character names change accordingly, with the exception of the author, whose character's name should always be Tim Crouch.

Music is present in the play as a release valve. It brings us into the here and now and helps the audience to feel good about being together. It is a treat! It can play for a long time without anything happening.

An audience facing an audience in two banks of seats.

No stage area in between.

An easy, playful presence.

No sense and every sense of a play beginning.

Blank underscoring (_____) represents the names of any number of audience members that ADRIAN has effortlessly and gracefully elicited and learned. We should get to know quite a few names over the course of the play.

There is freedom in ADRIAN's speech to improvise if needed.

Space.

ADRIAN: I love this. This is great, isn't this great? I
            love this! This! All this! When I came in –
            When I came in and saw this, just this, and
            I thought, Oh Wow! Didn't you? Did you?
            Maybe you didn't. Maybe you thought Oh
            Jesus! Did you? Oh Jesus Christ, maybe!

Space.

            This is such a versatile space. Isn't it
            versatile? It's amazing what they can do.
            They can do anything. Can't they?

Space.

            I'm Adrian. I'm Adrian and you are? Hello!
            What's your name? Do you love this,
            _____? Our knees touching! Don't you?
            Who'll you be next to. I'm next to you!
            What's your name? That's beautiful. You're
            beautiful! Isn't _____ beautiful? Everyone?

            I'll shut up. I'll stop.

            Someone else go!

Space.

Is everyone all right?

Are you?

Space.

What are we supposed to do, I wonder? Do you know?

Sounds good, doesn't it?

Does it?

I have some cuttings in my bag. I have a preview in the Metro/a review in the Standard! I see everything I do. You can't keep me away. Shall I read you it? Here, let me read it. It's not as though anything's happening, is it! It's not as though we're going to miss anything!

Here.

ADRIAN reads from a newspaper – a review or a preview of this play.

Yes, blah. Yes, well! Doesn't say anything really! Does it?

Space.

Everyone's looking at me! My face isn't ready for this level of attention! Don't look at me! Don't!

I've only just had the stitches out!! The bandages off! Look! Almost good as new!

Space.

Oh, we're all so gorgeous, aren't we? Look at us. Look!

I think we're better looking than the actors, don't you? Do you, _____? Do you? Look at us. Look. We're gorgeous.

Maybe not better looking... But more realistic! More chance of a snog from one of us than from the Prince of Denmark, don't you think! Do you, _____?

And you *are* looking at the kind of man who likes to hang around the stage doors! Don't you, _____? I waited for ages for Ralph Fiennes once after some French play. An incurable romantic, I am. I can't help it! Aren't you? _____? No? All that glamour? I can't resist it!

Making up for a thoroughly normal life. Do you have a normal life, _____? Do you? What do you do? That's fantastic! Isn't that fantastic? Not normal at all? Is it? What about you? What do you do? That's fantastic, too! Isn't it?

I think it is.

Space.

Oh, we're gorgeous.

But I often think – I think – I think that sometimes the most fantastical – the most made up thing in the theatre is us! Don't you, _____? I saw a play last year. And I remember thinking, 'that writer has imagined me'. I've been imagined! Poorly imagined! The audience has been badly written.

We're all going to have to *pretend ourselves!* Do you know that feeling, _____?

Space.

> And the actors just go on and on and on, don't they? About the state of the world or why they can't get laid. Or they smash each other's brains in! And we just let them, don't we? That's what we expect of them, isn't it _____. It's what we love, isn't it. We wouldn't be here. No one ever asks them to stop, do they? And the lights flash on and off and there's loud music and shouting.
>
> I can't do flashing lights!
>
> And everything's always so promising before the play begins! Before they open their mouths. That's the best moment, _____. We're all so expectant. We're all being so lovely! And then the lights go down.
>
> There's always hope, isn't there, _____. Hope is what brings us back, isn't it? Again and again and again. The hopeful moment! Are you hopeful, _____? Where are you with hope, _____?
>
> Without hope, what is there? Do you agree, _____?
>
> Look at us. Look at all our lonely, hopeful hearts!! Sitting here. Staring out! Hoping for something to happen. Waiting for someone to talk to us. Really talk.

An audience member in the middle of a block gets up and leaves. They are helped to leave by an usher.

> You say something then!

The door closing.

> You say something.

A beat.

Music plays.

Houselights go out, one by one, slowly, visibly. The audience becomes beautifully lit, slowly, visibly. Their light contained on them, with darkness all around.

Music stops.

Space.

TIM: I'm led downstairs by a young woman with her hair pulled back and held in place with a large plastic tortoiseshell hair grip – like sharp teeth chomping down on the back of her head! Ha! She's wearing a dress that makes her look a little like a nurse. She looks really clean. Like she'd smell really clean. I think about her being naked. Even at this time, in this state, I think about her naked and stretched out for me! Can you imagine? I look at the shape of her breasts. I think about the weight of her breasts.

She asks if I have ever used a floatation tank before and I say no. I say that this was a gift. I was given a token as a gift. A voucher. From the theatre, I tell her, as if she might be even remotely interested. The sound designer gave us tokens on the last night of a play I wrote, I say! I'm Tim Crouch, I tell her, the author. She looks blank. She hasn't heard of me! The sound designer of the play, I say, my play, said we looked like we all needed some sensory deprivation! It's taken me three months to redeem it!

I've been looking forward to it, I say. Ha ha. I talk too much when I'm nervous!

My mouth is dry.

Space.

She shows me the tank. It's sitting in the
middle of the room like an oversized
sarcophagus. She opens it up – lifting two
flaps at the near end, like trapdoor hatches
that come to rest on their hinges facing up
to the ceiling. Her dress is pressed across the
curves of her young body. I imagine her legs
opening for me, her dress lifting up. Her soft
flesh opening up for me. I imagine I –

Space.

Is this okay?

Is it okay if I carry on?

Do you want me to stop?

Do you?

Do you?

Space.

The tank is moulded fibreglass – and the
water is maybe only a foot deep. She shows
me the light switch and the alarm button.
She says the water is at blood temperature.
Ha ha! At blood temperature! She says she
hopes I have a good time. I thank her and
she leaves me.

Space.

I'm sorry.

Someone else go.

Space.

VIC: Tim said, with a monologue, the most
        important thing is to know who you're
        speaking it to. To whom you're speaking it.
        Do you understand?

        You can't just say, oh, I'm speaking it to
        myself. Or, I'm thinking out loud. Or, I'm
        just talking to 'an audience' in 'a theatre'! You
        can't just pick a spot above the audience's
        head and deliver it into the middle distance!
        You have to give the audience a character,
        a relationship to you. Doesn't matter if you
        can't see them. Something has to be at stake
        for the audience. They have to maybe need
        convincing of something, or persuading of
        something or rousing or enlisting. Imagine
        them as a child or – or a confessor. Enlisting
        is a good one! I'm enlisting you! Or they
        need seducing or pleasuring. Pleasing, I
        mean. But do you understand? Then the
        relationship between me and the audience
        is alive, is real, not rhetorical but active.
        Something is at stake. Tim said you should
        get them to a point where they almost feel
        able to answer back. Or shout out.

        So, I'm, let's say, 'provoking' you! Or maybe
        'rousing', or 'stirring' or something!

        What do you think?

        Really.

        What do you think?

        Can you see all right?

Space.

TIM: There's music playing ever so quietly in
        the room. I take my clothes off, fold them,

hang them up. It says on the voucher I'm supposed to wear trunks but I haven't brought any. I didn't bring any. It doesn't matter anyway. I stand for a moment in front of a mirror above a sink. I look at myself, at the offending articles. Ha ha. The guilty party.

I reach into the pocket of my jacket and take out a pen and a pad of Post-it stickers. I rest the pad against the sink and write a note. My hand is shaking! I peel off the sticker and place it on the outside of the hatch of the tank.

I mount the two steps that take me over the threshold and then step down into the water. It feels warmer than blood, but then when have I ever stepped into a pool of blood? Really, ha ha ha? I am holding a small plastic box in my hand.

Inside the box is a sharp blade, a cutting blade, like a scalpel. The sharpest thing I could find in the house! In Jules's studio. In my wife's studio.

I hold on to the grips on either side and lower myself down. I reach up for the handles of the trapdoor hatches and bring them together, closed above my head. Like this.

(The author re-presents the action.)

Can you see?

I lie back in the warm salt solution and my body bobs up like a cork! It's wonderful! The light inside the tank is still on. I float there in suspension. The music they have been playing has faded out. I am gripped with panic, ha ha. I don't yet feel able to switch out the light. Not that there's anything to see. I tip my head forward and look down at my toes and then back up to the roof of my coffin!

Space.

VIC: I played the part of Pavol in the play. The father. The abuser in the title. Tim said at the audition that life has not been good to Pavol, and that Pavol has not been good to life! That's brilliant, I said, and laughed and hated myself for sounding like a middle class idiot, rather than the monster I hoped they'd employ me for.

I still think they made a mistake in the casting. I wouldn't hurt a fly, let alone rape one with a broken bottle!

I mean, look at me.

Listen to me.

Space.

TIM: Here I am, I think. The prize-winning playwright. Entombed in the basement of a building. On the outskirts of a city. On the day that there are tanks at the airport. There are soldiers being flown home in coffins. There are photographers outside my house. The celebrated author. His location unknown to his wife and children and to the world! The famous playwright. Darling of the universities.

The lights very slowly fade out.

Near darkness. Silence.

In the dim light.

ESTHER: Has anyone here ever marched against the war?

Anyone?

I remember the day the theatre marched against the war! Would you like me to tell you? Yes?

Would you?

Would you?

It was a West End or an Equity thing organised to go along with a public demonstration. An anniversary of the war starting. We were encouraged to go in bits of costume or make-up. Can you imagine! The cast of Mamma Mia, Lord of the Rings, Spamalot, Les Mis, Hairspray, The History Boys, Wicked, Stomp, Joseph, The Lion King! All those actors! Actors from all those shows – singing their songs and dancing. The Billy Elliot cast dancing! I was in High School Musical at that time – fresh from Drama Centre. I was only 21. We took our pom poms! Not everyone went, of course. Some people were opposed to it. And there were companies from the National and the non West End theatres – the Tricycle, the Bush, the Royal Court, the serious ones who looked down their noses at us! But we didn't care, anyway. Not then, on the march. We were having fun!

And look at me now – at the Royal Court Theatre!

Those of us who hadn't made their own banners were able to pick up ready-made ones from various posts along the route. The most popular was one with a picture of a dead girl from a recent bombing and the slogan, 'Not One More Death'. Do you remember that image? It was an amazing day. We sang 'We all live in a terrorist regime', to the tune of Yellow Submarine! In my High School skirt and pig tails! All those trained voices! No wonder we were on TV!

Of course everyone had to get away for the matinees.

There were banner collection points but people had just dropped them outside the underground. We weren't allowed to take them on public transport. There were piles of the banners and we had to walk over them to get to the underground. It was weird walking over the photograph of the dead girl. Her dead eyes staring up at us. I had real difficulties in the matinee, wanting to cry. About the war and the dead girl.

Space.

Would you like me to sing for you?

Would you?

Yes?

Would you?

When an audience member says 'Yes', she sings some of a song from a West End musical.

The lights fade up very slowly over her song.

Space.

VIC: Do I look like a monster?

  Do I?

  I mean I mostly play sports teachers! Or corrupt policeman. Or whatever they give me, I'm not complaining. I went through a period of playing gays. I played a psychotic gay on The Bill! My girlfriend got quite worried about me – kissing all those blokes! Maybe it's the hair that does it – makes people think I'm queer or hard or something. Or both! I can't do anything else with it.

ESTHER: I played the part of Eshna in Tim's play. The daughter. The abused.

VIC: I should get a wig.

Space.

TIM: I switch the light out.

Space.

ESTHER: It was the hardest role of my career.

TIM: And I'm crying. Like a baby. Ha ha! Poor taste! Howling like a baby!

ESTHER: My husband knows how I feel about theatre. He said there was no question I should do it. Don't think about the money, he said.

TIM: I think I want the young woman to hear me. Someone to hear me. To come and hold me and stop me. To climb inside here with me.

ESTHER: I love the live-ness of theatre. The relationship with the audience. I do too much telly.

TIM: My own warm salty water joining the warm
            salty water around me.

ESTHER: I don't do enough theatre.

TIM: I cry and cry and cry.

ESTHER: You've probably all seen me in a certain low-
            budget film about some teenagers.

            Yes?

TIM: I shiver in the warm.

ESTHER: Or on the television.

TIM: I want to press the button.

ESTHER: Or in the papers.

TIM: I want to stop this.

ESTHER: It was the hardest thing.

Music.

Space.

TIM: The play was a poem, really. A personal
            lament. The violence is there as an
            underscoring to the central relationship.
            The father and his daughter. The abuser and
            the abused. A way of getting the characters
            closer to each other, just a dramaturgical
            device, really. The violence is not the most
            important thing, which some of the reviewers
            seemed to suggest. But it can't be avoided. I
            mean look around us.

            Society is defined by its edges, isn't it? Not by
            its centre.

I think I'd become more and more absorbed by images from the edges. I think we all had! Just through everyday exposure, really. And a hunger to see what was going on. What had become possible in the world we lived in.

What had become recently possible.

Or possible again.

Riven flesh, severed limbs, decapitated heads.

Is that okay? Decapitated heads, ha ha.

Space.

ADRIAN: I always book my tickets right when the season is announced. You know. I booked for this ages ago. Did you? When did you? Do you get a concession? Do you mind me asking? How much did you pay? Do you mind saying? _____? Online? What about you, _____? Do you live near here?

TIM: I never felt it was surprising. It became a small hobby of mine – like stamp collecting, ha. Not a collector, but an assembling, an assemblager – placing image against image. I took it upon myself to look at images of abuse, at beheadings, for example! To follow all the links on my computer.

To download and transfer and assemble.

To explore how these pictures fashion our relation to one another. To assemble and reassemble. On stage, I suppose. To bombard myself with all the gory details! It was remarkably easy to find. Harder almost not to. My gorgeous wife asked how I could look at images like these, let alone in a theatre. How can we not? I replied. If we do not represent them then we are in danger of denying their existence.

She deals with all this by cooking fabulous meals and spoiling the children! That's her way of dealing with it.

The unbearable image.

Is that a fair way of putting it?

Space.

My god, when I think about it, we're incredibly lucky.

My god, we're blessed!

Space.

ADRIAN: I'm a 'Friend'! A Friend of the Royal Court Theatre! That's why I see everything. I might know nothing about it. I just agree to see everything. I book at the beginning of the season. I trust them. The people who run the theatre. I'm rarely disappointed. And...I get a discount! Yay! You get £5 off the top ticket prices and you get a newsletter, an email. And you can book tickets earlier than anyone else. Is anyone else a 'Friend'? Anyone here? _____? _____? Are you? Well done us! Hooray! We're friends! We're helping to secure the future of new writing.

Sorry. Sorry. I'll stop. You go. You go on.

Space.

ESTHER: The first question everyone would ask is, 'What's the blood made out of?'

TIM: My intention was to deliver a shock – to
                create a – an amateur war zone on the
                stage – like a physical blow. A simulation
                of a physical blow. To represent what was
                happening in the real world. To show what
                was happening. Not in my life, of course,
                thank god, I'm incredibly lucky. But what I
                perceived. What we all perceived. The ethics
                of the images we saw. To push that to the
                extreme.

                Art operates in the extreme.

                And, of course, I was angry because we were
                at war. But it didn't have to be the war.

Space.

ESTHER: 'What's the blood made out of!'

ADRIAN: You should become Friends! Become a
                subscriber. Seriously. Everything they do
                here is good. Is great! It has an international
                reputation! I have a friend who lives in New
                York but he sees everything here. We don't
                know how lucky we are to have this on our
                doorstep. British theatre is the best in the
                world.

TIM: You know how a stubbed toe can sometimes
                release the flood-gates! The unexpectedness
                of physical injury – a slap or a knock. You
                didn't know you felt that way, but then a
                knock or a slap, er, reveals how you feel.

Music.

Space.

ADRIAN: The title of the play referred to the girl in it,
                I suppose. It was her face on the poster, in

the brochure – looking dreadful. Although it was more about the father and the war or whatever. I knew her because I'd seen her before – in that film where she was the girl. I didn't know him, though, the father. I thought he was marvellous. And of course I knew of the writer – who was also directing.

TIM: Or even missing the bottom step can invoke a feeling of incensed outrage at the invasion of the physical – into our ordered little world! Our protected little lives. You know?

ADRIAN: I'd wanted to see the first night, the press night. I love the press nights and as a Friend it's sometimes possible to get tickets because mostly, for the press night, they just go to the press and invited, you know, guests! Not plebs like us! But I was ill that time and they offered me another date. I was still ill, but I was determined to see it before the run ended, so I went on the last night. I shouldn't have gone. I knew there were flashing lights. It said it in the theatre. On signs in the theatre. Flashing lights and nudity. I'm a delicate flower! I blame it on myself.

ESTHER: 'What's the blood made out of!'

ADRIAN: I'm a lot better now. Don't you think? Look! I can see now. All better! There was a moment when they thought I'd lose an eye. A detached retina! A fractured socket. Sounds gruesome, doesn't it! But I'm really fine now. I really am! Don't you think, _____?

TIM: Here I am, a civilised man, a theatregoer. A writer.

31

ADRIAN: I missed the last fifteen minutes, didn't I?
            But I thought it was amazing anyway. So
            powerful. Really intense. Too intense. In such
            a small space and no air and all that gory
            stuff. And there was air conditioning! It was
            amazing! The critics couldn't make up their
            mind, but I wouldn't have missed it. I loved
            it.

            The actors were so brave!

            Did anyone else see it?

A sudden black out.

Space.

Lights up.

VIC: I thought they'd give it to someone foreign,
            Pavol. A real foreign actor. I'm Welsh, but...

            At the audition, we read from the play and
            Tim asked if I was okay about being in
            something like that, having to do the things
            my character has to do – you know, the sex
            and violence. He said:

TIM: Your agent said she thought you'd be okay.

VIC: I'm an actor!

            I didn't tell them that I hadn't worked for a
            year!

            Before rehearsals began we did some work
            on the accents and I spent a week with Tim –
            just exploring the character of Pavol. Didn't
            we?

TIM: Yes.

Space.

ESTHER: I played the part of Eshna in Tim's play.

Space.

TIM: In rehearsal we all watched a mobile phone
            film of some soldiers taking it in turns to
            rape a prisoner. To make her pregnant. It was
            posted on a website. Can you imagine? That
            I can tell you that we watched that? That I'm
            here, telling you that! Can you believe that?

            I rewrote quite a bit after that!

ESTHER: I played the part of the daughter.

TIM: Am I right? Look around you and tell me
            that this world is not full of horrors. Look
            around you.

            Look.

            Look.

            Can you see all right?

Space.

ESTHER: I couldn't do any of the early preparation
            before rehearsals because I was having a
            baby! Or rather, I had had a baby and I
            wanted to be with him as long as possible
            before I went back to work.

ADRIAN: What's his name?

ESTHER: His name's Finn. He's eight months now. I
            have a photograph of him. Would you like to
            see him?

            Would you?

            Yes?

Would you?

She shows a couple of photographs – passes them around.

He's beautiful, isn't he?

I'd worked with Tim before, hadn't I?

TIM: Yes.

ESTHER: I did a play of his at Soho. We'd got on
              really well – quite intense, really. I was going
              through a really hard time and he was great.
              A couple of years ago. Before my film came
              out. Before I married Paul. I'd got to know
              his family. I'm friendly with his family, his
              wife, Jules. Tim really wanted me for the
              part. He even named the character after me!
              And he was great about my situation, the
              baby. My concern was that I wasn't young
              enough for the part. She's meant to be
              sixteen.

Space.

VIC: We spent a lot of time on the computer
              – watching reports, understanding the
              situation. Looking at images. Some people
              said that the things that happened in the play
              were too extreme, but they're nothing to
              what we looked at.

              We even took a cheap flight and actually
              spent a couple of days over there. It's still a
              dangerous place. Tim wrote about the trip
              for the *Guardian* and was taking photographs
              for his blog.

              We kept on saying, 'There's a Pavol!' and
              'There's Pavol!' It was amazing. Life is totally
              brutal there. The effects of the war. Young

men with deformities pushing themselves around on skateboards. Without their shirts, so you see the open wounds or the twisted spines. Like Cardiff on a Friday night!

Tim talked about the play – about violence in a culture, about what happens to you when you live with that violence around you all the time. About how we have to recognise it, confront it, absorb it. We have to show it. He talked about how the human body is distorted, no – what was your word?

TIM: Abstracted.

VIC: Abstracted. Abstracted by the violence. I don't know. To be honest, I must say that I never really understood. But it's not my job to understand. I didn't write it. It's not the kind of play I'd go and see.

ESTHER: I've always looked younger than I am. But having a baby. Tim said that he wouldn't feel happy about a real young girl doing it – being exposed to those things. He said that the public would not be comfortable about that. That he would get the theatre into trouble.

VIC: We looked at the people. Tim talked about how the violence of the culture is shown in the bodies of the people we saw – the way they sit – like this. Or the way they hold their anger and despair. I understood this. As an actor, I understood this. I work through the physical. From the outside in.

In here, in the shoulders like this. Moving like this. Their arms like this.

He performs an action with his shoulders. ESTHER joins in.

Do you want to try that?

Everything we did was to help to tell the story.

ESTHER: Is everyone okay? Can you all see okay?

VIC: We went out one night, away from the hotel. With a guide who carried a gun! We talked to some men. In the back room of an underground bar that our guide had organised. I really found Pavol there, I suppose. One man, whose family had been killed in one of the massacres. Whose son had been stood against a wall with other men from the village and shot. By the militia or someone. He showed me an old photograph of his son. And I brought that man back with me to London! In my overhead luggage, Tim said! Took him into the rehearsal room. Shared him with the production team.

It was the most useful thing.

Lights fade out.

Space.

Lights up.

ESTHER: On the first day of rehearsals Tim gave us jobs to do. Didn't you?

We had to go out into the city and find someone who connected with the themes of the play. We had to study them and interview them and then bring back what we'd observed. It was brilliant because we'd done loads of that kind of stuff at Drama Centre. I went to a shelter for women who had suffered domestic violence. I was really lucky. I met a woman who had been raped as a teenager by her father. That's just like my character, I said!

Space.

VIC: But it's the quality of the writing, you know? It's not me, it's the writing. You know it's well written when it gets inside you. It really got inside me. There's only so much research you can do as an actor, but if it's not backed up by the writing.

You know?

Space.

ESTHER: Her name was Karen. She was like this. Can you see that? Her tension here. Her eyes like this. A filthy track suit.

Space.

TIM: Hello Karen.

ESTHER: Yeah.

TIM: Thanks for agreeing to talk with us.

ESTHER: I'm not –

TIM: It's okay. We're just really pleased that you could be here with us. Aren't we? We just wanted to get to know you, really, to hear a little bit about you. We're really interested in you, aren't we? Aren't we?

VIC: Yes!

ESTHER: Yeah?

TIM: Do you want to talk about what happened to you? About why you're here?

ESTHER: What?

TIM: In this place.

ESTHER: In the shcl'cr?

TIM: In the shelter or in the theatre. It's up to you.
             Wherever you want to be.

ESTHER: I don't wanna be 'ere.

TIM: That's fine! We're not here! We can be
             wherever you want!

ESTHER: Don't fuckin' wanna be 'ere.

VIC: That's fine.

TIM: Do you want to talk about your dad?

ESTHER: No.

TIM: We understand. It won't go any further than
             this. Do you want to tell us about what he
             did? What he made you do?

ESTHER: No.

             Stuff.

TIM: What kind of stuff?

ESTHER: Stuff.

TIM: Did he hurt you?

ESTHER: I ain't a fucking kid.

VIC: It's all right, Karen.

ESTHER: I ain't a fucking kid.

TIM: Of course.

ESTHER: Films and pictures and stuff.

TIM:	What?
ESTHER:	What do you fuckin' think?
TIM:	I know how difficult this must be for you.

Space.

	Do you want to carry on?
ESTHER:	I never –
TIM:	And what did he do?
ESTHER:	He put things – filmed me with his mates. Putting things inside me. What you fucking think he did? Read me fucking story books?
TIM:	I'm so sorry.
ESTHER:	No you're not. You're not fucking sorry. None of you are fucking sorry.
VIC:	How old were you when it started, Karen?
ESTHER:	–
TIM:	How old, Karen?
ESTHER:	Twelve.
VIC:	Twelve.
TIM:	How did that make you feel, your dad doing those things?
	Karen?
ESTHER:	Can we stop, Tim?

Space.

TIM:	Would anyone else like to ask Karen any questions?

You're happy to improvise, aren't you, Esther?

ESTHER: –

TIM: Are you okay about that, Karen? If other people ask you some questions?

ESTHER: –

TIM: Anyone? Would anyone else like to ask Karen any questions?

Anyone?

Maybe some questions are asked of Karen by members of the audience.

ADRIAN: I'd like to ask a question.

TIM: Of course.

ADRIAN: What was it like working with Daniel Craig?

ESTHER: I never had any scenes with him, really.

TIM: This is Karen we're asking, not Esther.

I think we should thank Karen for coming in and Esther for bringing her.

They clap 'Karen'.

Space.

More Space.

VIC: We worked on the world of the play and the relationships. It was harrowing sometimes – pushing ourselves deeper and deeper into the truth of it. The relationship between Pavol and his daughter. The manipulation and abuse. Improvising and improvising. And then working on the text. Working to establish the contact between the characters

– the psychological action. Finding the truth of the story in each moment.

ESTHER: I'm not saying that my character was Karen. It wasn't an impersonation. I think that if she had come to see the play she wouldn't have recognised herself. It was just incredibly helpful to have her as – as a reference point.

VIC: The guy we met over there. I was hot-seated as him, in the rehearsal room here! Just here, by the side of the building. I had to physically bring him in, in me. I smashed a table, do you remember? That poor stage manager, Nicky, was in tears! She spent ages finding that rehearsal table! And I wanted to apologise to her and Tim said, don't apologise, Pavol wouldn't apologise. Do you remember?

TIM: Yes!

VIC: Tim was amazing – he would push me to places I didn't know were inside me. Esther, who played Eshna my daughter, was terrified sometimes. Weren't you?

ESTHER: Yes!

VIC: I perfected this dead look behind the eyes. It was mentioned in the reviews. Like this! I can't do it now, but it used to really upset my girlfriend. See? This? See? She almost called the police once. She almost called the police! Something she felt had gone too far one time. She said I had gone too far. But I couldn't leave Pavol in the rehearsal room. I couldn't leave him on stage. I really tried! He would come home with me. 'Leave me alone!'

Space.

ESTHER: But I think that's why the play was so
             successful. Or so powerful. The audience
             could see that we'd done our research,
             you understand, they believed us. The
             fear looked so real. They left the theatre
             absolutely stunned. In shock! Tim would
             come in every now and then during the
             run, wouldn't you, and was unbelievably
             encouraging. He would illuminate depths to
             the meanings.

Space.

VIC: She said it had changed me. That I wasn't the
             man that she knew.

TIM: You write and write and discover and
             discover. And then you let go. You hand
             over. You leave it to the actors. They will
             make their own discoveries. You leave it to
             your audience.

VIC: I had lost my joy.

TIM: There were a lot of ideas in my head. A lot
             of images. My job was to find a story that
             would contain those ideas, those questions. A
             relationship. That's the job of a writer. Not to
             go in and solve things. But to reveal things,
             things for other people to solve. To present
             the truth of the story.

VIC: I wasn't fun any more.

Space.

ESTHER: Oh, yes! We spent a lot of time with a special
             effects guy from a film studio. And Malcolm
             the fight director.

TIM: It wasn't my story.

ESTHER: Malcolm was amazing.

TIM: Some people thought, I suppose, that maybe
            I had experienced things like that – in my
            childhood. But nothing could be further from
            my truth! Ask Jules. I had researched them,
            but my job is to represent them, not to have
            lived them.

ESTHER: I had pouches of stage blood strapped to bits
            of my body. One famous moment when Vic
            would hit me in the face and blood would
            spray from my eye. I had a sponge in my
            hand, so when I brought my hand up like
            this – like this, can you see? – I could make
            the blood spray out. Nobody knew how it
            was done! It was really shocking and real.
            The stage was a mess at the end of the show.
            Poor old stage management spent hours
            clearing it up at the end. I had to shower for
            ages to get it all off me!

TIM: Confronted by the death of his wife.
            Confronted by his daughter in the ruins
            of his home. His daughter who demands
            from him a new start, a fresh perspective.
            A salvation. The younger generation
            demanding change from the older.
            Something which cannot be accomplished.
            Which is why he starts to abuse her, brutalise
            her, mutilate her.

ESTHER: And a bag strapped to my inner thigh – here
            – with raw liver in it. So when Vic reached
            his hand up inside me and tears away at my
            womb – he just reached into that bag. My
            god, people would gasp at that moment,
            groan, faint!

TIM: The play was a psychological study. It's not meant to be taken literally. It's an allegory.

Space.

A brilliant light-show plays across the audience.

Space.

ADRIAN: Would anyone like a Malteser? _____? I haven't got enough for everyone.

ADRIAN hands out a few Maltesers to the people whose names he has come to know.

This is the safest place in the world! Don't you think, _____? Safe, in here? Where are you with safety? I mean, nothing really happens in here, does it? Not really. Nothing real.

I get here and I go flop! I go, phew! It feels like in here anything is possible and it's safe. It's all safe! I've seen everything imaginable here. I've seen bum sex and rimming and cock sucking and wankings and rapings and stabbings and shootings and bombings. Bombings and bummings!! I've seen someone shit on a table! I've seen a man have his eyes sucked out. I've seen so many blindings! And stonings. Um. I've seen a dead baby in a bag. A baby stoned to death. I've seen a dead baby get eaten! That was great!

It's such an education! Isn't it? Isn't it, _____?

And nobody knows! Nobody knows! The cars and buses go round and round outside and none of them have any idea. No idea at all. That we're here, in here, safe in here, enjoying our Maltesers and our bum sex. It's a private club for the depraved!! Don't you think, _____? There's no danger of it going any further because we're all consenting adults. All of us, all us dirty mother-fucking cunts!!

I'm sorry. That's a horrible thing to say! Sorry. Sorry. Sorry. I'm sorry. I'm sorry. Sorry.

Quite free-ing, though!

And it doesn't matter. It doesn't matter anyway because nobody out there knows and nobody out there really cares. Do they?

Oh, I love this.

So on the last night of the run I saw the play. Well, saw *most* of the play! Who was it who said that – some critic – 'sodomy and vomit'!

TIM: The press were pretty good, really. They had nothing but praise for the two actors. Some failed to get the poetics, really. They all commented on the visceral, er, experiential quality of the writing. And, of course, the more gruesome aspects of the production. On the whole, though, positive. We were sold out almost before we opened. A lot of them had come to see Esther, I think. There had been an article about her in a Sunday newspaper.

Space.

ESTHER: He's an American contractor. An engineer, Tim said. The man is kneeling up, slightly to the right as we're looking at it – left of

45

the camera. I suppose if you looked for it you would say he looks tired. But you don't think about things like this when you see him because your heart is in your mouth. You only notice these things after you've watched it a number of times.

We saw maybe 15 different ones. Over and over. We had to go away and find them. And we'd recreate them in rehearsal. For the end of the play.

TIM: I would pop in and out of the run – to see how they were coping. Sit and watch. Meet up with Vic and Esther afterwards, give a few notes. Hearing stories of audience responses – standing ovations, faintings! I think our work in rehearsal really paid off.

ESTHER: One where the hostage is just shot unexpectedly and everyone in the frame jumps out of their skin. It's almost funny. Maybe the gun went off by mistake, but the man's head is blown apart.

One with a sword like they do in Saudi Arabia – with the man crying and crying and begging for his life – an Italian – and two men having to almost lie down on the floor on either side to hold him upright.

This image of the engineer is held for some time – just the sound of the birds and the child occasionally – or maybe not a child. I don't know. I don't know. It could be a television on somewhere. There's a sense of expectation. It doesn't feel like a place where this will happen, you know. The American contractor doesn't know where to look. At one point he looks at the camera. Maybe he doesn't know it's on. Maybe he doesn't know what's going to happen.

Are you all okay?

Are you okay if I carry on?

Space.

ADRIAN: I sometimes wonder what it would be like to be an actor in one of those things – you know. Don't you? I mean they're not really having their bum fucked or their cock sucked, are they? Are they? We know that! And there are two hundred people watching them whist they pretend that they are. I wonder if they ever get a bit – you know? I wonder what goes through their mind? So how does that feel? What does that do for their self-esteem, _____? Do you know what I mean? How do they feel when they wake up in the morning?

'Have a good day at work, darling! Be careful when you eat that baby!' And getting paid for it. What's that like, I wonder. Do they have any say in it?

Space.

ESTHER: And then the third terrorist or soldier goes behind the American contractor and he holds the American contractor's head back and the American contractor lets out a gasp and the terrorist is screaming at the camera and he hacks the knife into the man's throat.

VIC: I should have talked to someone during the run.

ESTHER: This one more than any of the others.

VIC: I really went to pieces during the run.

ESTHER: I don't know why.

VIC: I remember taking my girlfriend to a
              restaurant after one performance – you
              know, just down here on the King's Road,
              where they come and cook at your table.
              And the chef, the Japanese chef, accidentally
              splashed me with hot oil and I just flipped
              and pushed him to the ground. There was no
              release at the end of the play. It just balled up
              and up. Tighter and tighter.

Space.

ESTHER: I wanted to throw up, go outside. But we had
              to watch it. Nothing else existed in the room
              apart from that thing. Do you understand?

VIC: My girlfriend said that the theatre should pay
              for us both to have counselling – to deal with
              post traumatic stress! I told her don't be daft!
              It was my problem, my thing. It was only a
              play!

ESTHER: And it happened there, in a room in Chelsea.
              That beheading. With us all gathered around
              the laptop. On a coffee break while we
              were working on Act Two. That's where it
              happened. What were we doing? There. In
              Chelsea. Here. Just here. Just to the side of
              this building. Just past stage door.

Space.

VIC: At the end of each performance we would
              leave the theatre from the stage door and
              there would always be people there. And on
              the last night, Tim had come round to the
              dressing room with a bottle. We all drank

quickly – on empty stomachs! And the
artistic director of the building came to thank
us. And there was a card for each of us from
the sound designer with the vouchers, and
a note from him saying that he thought we
could all do with a bit of sensory deprivation.

ESTHER: I said to Tim, why are we watching this?

VIC: And really I just wanted to leave.

ESTHER: And at that moment music starts to play –
            Arab music. Really loud.

VIC: My girlfriend was very glad when the run
            finished.

ESTHER: And it's terrible. Not the music, but the
            whole thing. And whoever it is is cutting into
            the American's throat. Slicing and hacking.
            And the American is, I suppose, is what you
            would say spasming – jerking. His whole
            body.

            Like this.

ESTHER performs the actions. She invites the audience to do the same.

            Do you want to do this?

VIC: Tim and I left together. Isn't that right?

TIM: –

VIC: And I left the theatre and there was a crowd,
            mostly waiting for Esther because of the film,
            but also fascinated because of what they'd
            just seen, and it was the last night of the run
            and there'd been so much publicity and
            so crowding around. But not really saying
            anything – a little shocked still I think. No
            one really recognised Tim, of course, but

everyone looked at me. I'd been terrorising them for the last hour and a half! And it's the last night and I'm just wanting to go, to get into the underground and go. But there are people everywhere. Their faces. Staring at me. And it's dark.

ESTHER: And this is a man. Not a goat, or a pig, but a man, a man with a wife whom we read about in the Observer, with children, a family.

VIC: And then I am approached by someone – someone – someone – who comes too close. Doesn't he? Would you say, Tim? Tim?

TIM: –

VIC: Too close for that moment, anyway, at the end of that show, at the end of the run. With me wanting to get away. And his speech is slurred and his movement is awkward. He seems to trip towards me and is saying something I can't quite make out.

The following three speeches are overlapped.

ADRIAN: I'm so sorry. Sorry I made such a nuisance. I feel terrible. How do you feel? /How does it feel?

VIC: And I put my hand out to keep him away / and he seems to grab hold of it and I think he looks as if he's about to hurt me.

ADRIAN: I thought you were brilliant. You're beautiful. Thank you so much! It's such an amazing play. Sorry I ruined it.

VIC: And then I just lash out.

ESTHER: We put articles on the rehearsal wall. And photographs. Oh God, one photograph of a

man whose head had been driven over by a
tank. Seriously. Just flat and crushed. It was
almost funny. Like stepping on a carton of
drink.

VIC: And the crowd take a step or two back. And
        seem to create an arena. Tim steps back
        too. And I look at this man who I think
        is attacking me, and I defend myself. He
        clings to me and I start to kick him off me.
        I'm convinced my life is in danger and so I
        start to kick him. You know? I don't stop to
        think. Do you understand? It's not hard to
        understand. Tim? Tim?

ESTHER: I found it difficult to leave the house and get
        to performances. Not sleeping. Not enjoying
        my food. Not bearing to have anyone touch
        me. With Paul or Finn, or at my parent's
        even. Seeing things. On people's faces.
        Looking at Finn and his face is black from
        the bombing. Or when the supermarket
        delivery comes and I open the front door,
        I see the delivery-man with blood spurting
        from his throat.

VIC: Is it? He's attacking me. I'm being attacked.
        And so I kick and kick – to his legs, then, as
        he falls, to his body, then, as he's down, to
        his head. I could stop, but I continue. The
        crowd take another step back and just watch
        me. And Esther is there now, by the stage
        door.

ESTHER: And questioning what I was doing as a
        mother. Bringing a child into a world like
        this. Finding it hard to be with him, leaving
        him with other people while I took myself
        off. I suppose a bit of a breakdown.

VIC: And nobody does anything. And I kick and
             kick and kick. And I'm shouting, I suppose.
             Just like in the play. And everyone is
             watching. Just watching. Nobody tries to stop
             me. Nobody tells me not to. So I continue.

ESTHER   I think it's good to cry.

VIC: You cunt. You cunt. Cunt.

ESTHER: It's good to cry. I think it's good.

The intro of the West End musical song that ESTHER sang earlier starts to play.

             It means we're getting somewhere. It means
             we got somewhere. With the play. There
             were nights during the run when I would
             look out at the audience on the curtain call
             and see a sea of wet faces.

             There were nights when Vic and I would
             clap the audience. Out of gratitude. Gratitude
             that they'd put up with it all. That they
             hadn't walked out! I think if it had been us,
             we would have walked out. So we would clap
             them.

ESTHER starts to clap.

The song plays louder and louder.

VIC: Cunt. Cunt.

ESTHER continues to clap.

ADRIAN joins in the clapping.

             Cunt. Cunt.

VIC gets up and leaves the auditorium.

The music ends.

Silence.

TIM: We had a dinner party. Some time after the show had finished. Jules had slow cooked lamb and pomegranate and she made a Nigel Slater lemon meringue ice cream. Our big kids were staying with friends. We invited Andy and Karl, who directed this. And Vic of course with his girlfriend. And Esther and Paul – who had brought their baby, Finn. At that age it's easier to bring them with you. They sleep so soundly. They'd put Finn in a travel cot in the box room, my study. It was so lovely to see everyone. Such a great group of friends. Such good friends.

The lights start to fade out extremely slowly.

The meal was a sort of thank you to everyone for everything. A recognition that the project had been a rather special one. That everyone had really put themselves into it.

Vic had been questioned but the man hadn't pressed charges. In fact, he was very apologetic. He'd passed out towards the end of the show, passed out, fainted, fitted, I don't know. The flashing lights. The ushers had taken him out without disturbing the play. They'd been brilliant. He was taken to the bar and been given a cup of tea or something. He was okay. He'd hit his head, bit his tongue or something, which is why Vic was scared or disorientated. The man had blood on his face already when he approached Vic.

Vic was very upset about it. He apologised again to everyone that evening but we all

said don't think about it. Don't think about it.
No one blamed Vic. We know Vic's not like
that.

The lights are nearly out.

We all got drunk. Andy was staying on the
sofa in the front room. Karl went back to
Richmond. Esther and Paul crashed out
in the spare room. They were exhausted
with the baby, and Esther had been filming
some TV drama thing that day. Vic and his
girlfriend left at about 1am. Jules stacked the
dishwasher and took herself to bed.

A dim light remaining.

I pour a glass of malt whisky and go to my
study. I check my emails and then sit in front
of my screen and just meander, really, drift,
not really thinking. Not thinking. I type in
my password. I am tired but don't feel like
going to bed. Images of flesh! I'm not proud,
but we've all done it, haven't we? Haven't
we? Finn is fast asleep in the travel cot by my
side. It's a warm evening. I'm a bit drunk.
I feel myself getting big. My throat is dry. I
take myself out and just begin to gently fuck
myself, you know. We've all done that, at the
end of a long day. Haven't we? A couple of
clicks.

A couple of clicks before bed!

I see a baby. This baby has a dummy in its
mouth.

I have the choice to continue.

I have the choice to stop.

Everyone in the house is asleep apart from me. The baby's skin is damp with sweat from the evening heat, presumably, in this strange house. The image is grainy. The sound of voices from outside, maybe, from the street. A television on somewhere. The room is cramped and untidy. I'm a little shocked with myself.

I turn down the volume.

I decide to continue. Just like that. In a second. Less than a second.

Click. Click.

The baby's dummy is removed and I look at the shadow cast on it. I watch the penis just gently being placed against the baby's mouth and then slowly being pushed in. Not violently, actually. Actually quite gently. Quite lovingly.

I decide to continue.

Everything is muted. My heart is racing. I pull harder. This baby stirs but it does not wake. It does not wake. It has no idea what is going on. It has no idea. When I come, a small amount of cum goes on to the edge of my computer screen. I quickly wipe it off, wipe myself. And join Jules in bed, curling around her lovely warm body and kissing the back of her neck. I am asleep in seconds.

In my meanderings, I forget to log off, forget to shut down, to Delete History.

Of course, when Esther wakes early because her baby is crying. Crying in the box room.

Lights slowly fade up.

ESTHER gets up and leaves the auditorium.

> I thought about taking out my eyes. At first, I thought that would be the thing to do. The offending articles. Ha ha. The guilty party. But this is better. Less classical. Here in the dark. In this warm salt solution.
>
> I press the blade into my neck.
>
> Do I continue? The young woman will read the Post-It note. She'll know to call the police before she does anything else. My wife will not forgive me anyway.
>
> You won't forgive me, anyway. I know you. Look at you. You won't. You won't forgive me.
>
> Anyway.
>
> Nobody was hurt.
>
> Anyway.
>
> I apologise.
>
> Anyway.
>
> I continue.
>
> The writing is leaving the writer.

The death of the author.

TIM walks out of the theatre.

The houselights are on. The doors to the theatre are open.

The End.